LONG LOST

KAASHVI NIGAM

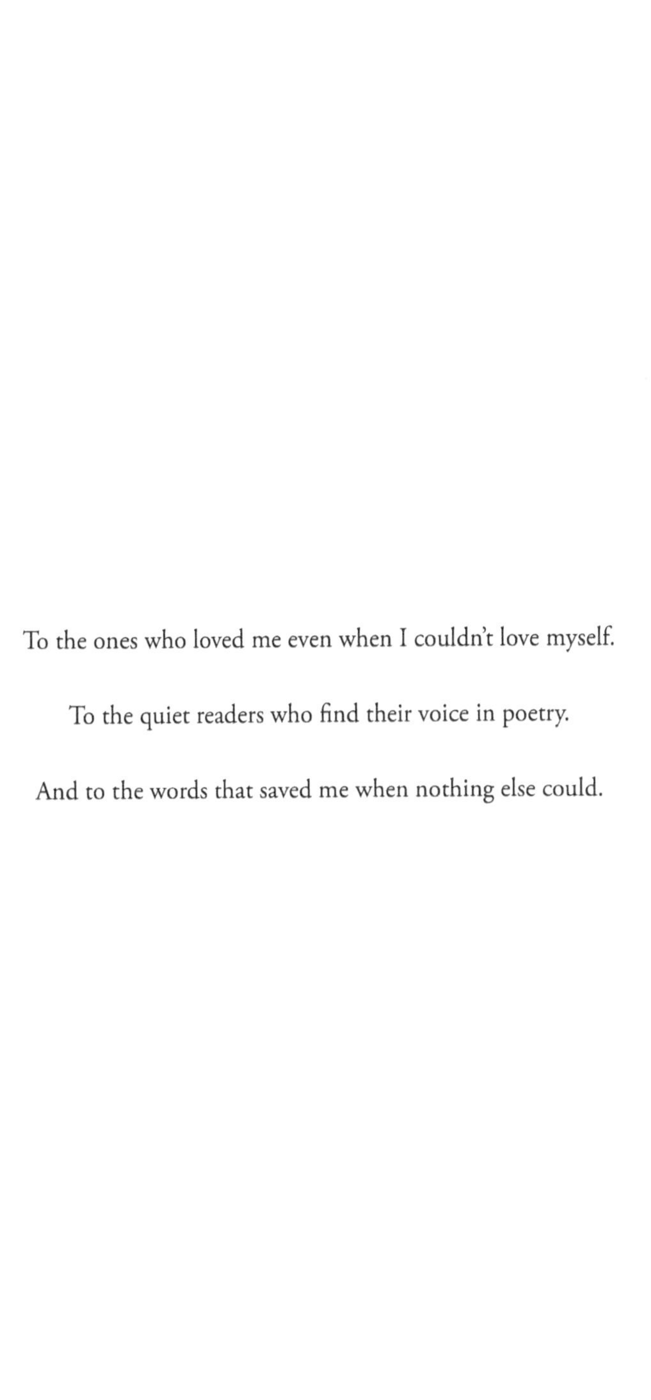

To the ones who loved me even when I couldn't love myself.

To the quiet readers who find their voice in poetry.

And to the words that saved me when nothing else could.

Contents

Contents

Contents

Foreword

I believe that anyone can relate to this anthology of my poems,
for all of us have gone through the cycle of love, loss, and life.
So maybe there are parts in the book you might like.
And if you do, keep it close and let the beauty of words sink into
your heart.

Let it bloom, no matter its colours.
If it's dull, give it a little love.
And if it's pale, give it a little sun,
but don't condemn it to another forgotten song yet to be sung.

I write this to all who may read this book.
These poems are a deep part of my soul, which has grown into the
ink of the pages you see.

You may like it, you may adore it, you may hate it,
but these are mine, in all their raw passion, ugly truth, and the glory
they have.

So, ladies and gentlemen,

I present to you,
the parts—broken and sewed—of Kaashvi Nigam's Body, Mind,
Heart, and Soul.

Preface

Inspiration for my art in this book has been taken from every soul I have met or heard of, from every movie I have watched, from every character I have read, and from every book I have kept close to my heart.

You need not go through the same situation to write about it; you just need to feel it.

I have felt all these emotions—of love, loss, and life— not through the times of my own living but through the ones I see, both in fiction and reality.

And that is the true inspiration of this book, "FICTION."

I have just taken the water from different waters and quenched your thirst in a different glass that I have made.

Acknowledgements

This book would not have been possible without the unwavering love and support of my family. To my friends who listened to my endless ramblings about poetry and never stopped believing in me—thank you. To the poets and writers who inspired me, your words became my guiding light. And finally, to every reader who picks up this book—you are the reason these words exist beyond my soul.

Thank you.

Prologue

to write poetry is to lay your soul barren infront of the world

and hope of letting the wildflowers grow

so i hope you'll not pluck them

rather let them bloom with the love you shall show.

1. The Silent Song of Poetry

Poetry, the rhythm of melancholy,

The sentences laced with assonance and repetition,

With deep words like the ocean.

But shouldn't poetry

Just be your feelings—

A string of words

That could never attach the world?

Shouldn't it be the silent song

That was never sung?

Shouldn't it be the loud thoughts,

Written with ink and blood?

2. The Fading Ink of Time

• 2 •

I fear the ink of my pen will dry,

that my pages shall fade.

I fear the rhymes will run away,

as they once had evade.

I fear, I shall reek of old parchment and the ink stains on my

floor.

I fear that my words will be condemned to a lore.

3. Floods of Feminity

I bleed and bleed for the children I never bore.
I carry this pain since I was a child, and so shall my daughters.

Rivers of agony flow through me,
bringing floods, disrupting my body—
and the world sits, not even acknowledging my misery.

My stomach twists and turns.
My body in a constant earthquake.

What shall I do with this gift,
which was given to me a bit too early?
This gift, whose name the world cannot even utter,
and yet I am supposed to be strong,
for in the future, I will be a mother.

It is not that I loathe this menses,
neither is this a curse,
but I loathe how the world wishes me to be an oak tree
when I am nurturing future flowers.

How they wish for me to burn like the sun,
when I am the cool breeze of the midnight moon.

How they wish for me to be the thunder of a storm,
but I am the chirping of the morning birds I see.

This time is aching,
but if provided silence, one can find peace.
And if only the world could understand this plea.

4. A Love I Couldn't Hold

And it's not that I didn't want to hold you.
I wanted to hold you for eternity.

But my hands—too cold,
my heart—a bit too old.

I was scared that I'd harm you,
that you'd leave me too.

I wanted to hold you tight,
like how the sky holds the starry night,
how my glass holds the perfect wine.

But maybe we were two different poles,
carrying in our hearts deep holes.

I can't hold you, my dear.
No matter how much I want to.
I can't.

So I bid you goodbye,
for you have set my heart on fire,

and I have turned yours into ice.

I will dream to hold you till my last breath,
till my demise.

5. Wildflowers on My Grave

I hope wildflowers grow on my grave,

They burst out of my ribs,

Where once was a beating heart.

I hope they cover my tombstone,

Devoiding me of all identity and past sin.

I hope they are beautiful,

As once I dreamed of death.

I hope they have thorns,

So they remain untouched,

Like the ghost of my lips.

I hope my place of rest is condemned

To a grave covered with wildflowers.

6. The Sun to your Moon

Did you see the moon tonight?

It nearly came close to your bright.

Did it make you smile?

Did it make you wish you stayed a while?

I saw how the moon embraced the stars,

Like how once we did with our beating hearts.

A tear slipped from my eye,

Knowing that I'm the sun in your sky—

Brightening you from afar,

But never close enough to become your star.

7. The Tragedy of Unknowing

"I never knew who I was
until I killed myself—
that is the greatest tragedy of my life."
she says.

"Who were you then?"
he asked.

"A corpse,
trying to dance
on a stage of beating hearts,
to the tune
of a dead man's bones clattering."
she whispered.

- an extract from a future book

8. Of Angels and Sins

The angels once whispered in my ears
That the devil resides in everyone's heart,
And the name of God on everyone's tongue—
So, I wondered, who was my Lord?

Was it the beating of my heart,
Or the words I spoke of God?
Always vacillating between the two,
Never knowing my true existence.

Was it my heart?
Was it my lips?
Was it the aching of my soul?

As I lay in my coffin,
Death gently holding my hand,
Where was my abode?
Or would I sink this boat?

I glance at myself in the mirror,
Pale and cold as ever.
I looked inside my heart and mind—
Neither God nor devil I find.

But then I looked into my eyes,
And I saw it all—
How God and I reached the top of the cliff,
And in the end, the devil pushed me.
Into the pit, I fall.

The angels who once whispered softly
Now laughed and mocked.
And I still didn't know—
Who was the devil, and who was God?

Betrayed, I lay in pain,
Broken on the floor in vain,
My blood cascading down my skin.
I realized I was a girl
With no hope, love, or kin.

Death looked at me, waiting for the poison kiss,
But where would I go?
To the verity, or back to my sins?

I closed my eyes and opened them again,
Only to see that not even death
Was my friend.

In rage, I sob and cry,

Not knowing who I am or why.
I smear my blood upon my face—
Now I wasn't part of their prayer or grace.

I wasn't with the good or evil,
I wasn't white or black.
I was like the earth with her cracks.

I didn't belong to the devil or God,
To myself, I belonged.
My heart and mind were neither of theirs—
I was the monarch of my kingdom with no heirs.

I was now on my own,
Not lost, but alone.
Now I had let go of the blind,
And the whole world I find.

Now, there was no devil in the peace of night,
Nor was there any water holy and pure.
There was just myself—
My skin, my bones, my heart, my soul—
In love, and in no need of a cure.

9. The Forgotten Mug

And here it goes again
I am like an old mug
You use me every single day
But when something special comes
You hide me away

I know you're fond of me
I've stayed this long
But you'll think for hours to say
"Why don't you come along?"

And I'm just waiting
around the corner
Waiting for you warm me up
So I don't get called a "loner"

I wish to be filled with love
The love which I seek everyday
Where you fill me up to my brim
and sip it with your lips
and say
"I wish this moment would never go away"

10. November's Embrace

November -

The month of memories, poetry, and being alone.

The month where you feel warm even when it's cold.

The month where you're excited for a new story

While missing the ending of this one.

The month where you long to write poems

Of love and sorrow,

The month where you wish

There was a bit more love to borrow.

11. Whispers of the Waves

I am in love with waves,
but they also give me scares.
They are sometimes strong, sometimes low—
they come slow,
and fast, they go.

They bring gifts from the ocean,
laying them on the sand,
like fingers tracing a new land,
like flowers having their first stand.

But as they leave, they take serenity and gifts,
leaving the sandy land,
returning to their bliss, their home.
They leave behind an essence of love,
they leave you alone.

These waves are like love.
These waves are like home.

At first, they might seem revolting,
but as my warm skin collides with the cold, crystal hue,

it feels like a visit to love was due.

They provide immense care,
they love but also show despair.
They shine beneath the sun and moon,
smiling whether it's hot or cool.

Yet, they cry and rage as mighty waves—
for they, too, are sometimes scared.

Waves—simple enough to understand,
beautiful enough to love,
soothing enough to be sunk in,
melodious enough to be sung.

Strong enough to fear,
yet
glorious and vast enough to be shared.

12. Sweet Abyss of You

I don't need water to drown
I can engulf myself into your honey sweet voice
And dive in your ocean words
And still not feel like dying or
out of breath.
Like a drug which is numbing
And making me feel alive
at the same time
Your voice is like the hot mug of
chocolate.
It provides me immense warmth while holding it
And even more so much sweetness into this bitter world

13. Fifteen's Maze

Being fifteen
is like a nightmare,
not a dream.
It's not only the changes
of my body,
it's the changes
of my surroundings.
It's the creepy man
who has started to stare,
or the teachers now
separating genders by chairs.
It's being mature
while being scolded like a child.
It's now the family jokes
about me being a bride.
It's the lectures to be
wary of boys.
It's being told
there is no space for toys.
It's the new subjects
that I must choose.
It's about finding a career,
not my muse.

It's about preserving
the family's name.
It's about being a pawn,
not the game.
It's about being strong and bold,
while having no one for you to hold.
It's about the unsaid feelings,
now locked in a cage.
It's the confusion of life,
like being stuck in a maze.
It's about finding solace in a book,
while knowing how to cook.
It's about respecting elders
and being quiet when you're right.
It's about finding pieces of yourself
and holding them tight.
It's about finding wonder and magic
in everything,
and letting yourself
show your feelings.
It's not about hating yourself
or your surroundings.
It's about thinking the world's upside down
and sometimes acting like a clown.
It's about loving and being free.
It's about living with care,
not misery.

Being fifteen
might be a nightmare,
but I'm going to
live it like a dream.

14. Blue and Its Rue

There is a lot of sadness in the world, I wonder—
For the sea is blue,
So is the sky.
Is the ocean filled with the tears of sorrow,
Or does the sky wish for a bit more revel?
But shouldn't blue be the colour
Of freedom and depth?
For there is nothing deeper than the sea,
And nothing as boundless as the sky.
Blue is the colour of indulgence,
Of the vastness of feelings,
And the tranquility of the indefinite.

15. The Storm and Quiet Sea

Your body is like the calm sea,

Mine is like a tsunami.

We are the same,

Yet—

We are different.

Our souls may be alike,

But our hearts will never know each other's name.

Your heartbeat is the soft rain

Pattering against my bedroom window,

Whilst mine is the throbbing thunder.

We both carry a deep mind

And a passionate heart,

But mine is heavy with agony,

And yours with wonder.

16. Fading Echoes of Beauty

So many words, lost between pages,
And so many books, lost between the ages.
My heart aches when I think of the beauty lost—
No, not just the one people nowadays buy at a cost.
But beauty that once resided in people's minds,
The kind that lived in the soul—one of a kind.
And now?
Now, it's shimmer, the glam, the silhouettes—
Perfection framed on magazine covers.
Now, it's about sculpting bodies, not hearts,
To find a lover.
We have caged the wildness, the beauty of it all,
In a tiny prison wrapped in gold.
We have let love, beauty, body, soul, and mind
Be measured, bought, and sold.

17. Crossroads of Fate

I stand here on this crossroad,
alone and afraid.

To choose one path
is not in my fate.

But alas, the world again tells me—
"*It's a choice everyone makes,
so come join the rat race.*"

But on one road, my heart beats,
the other, it stops.
On one road, my tongue sings tales,
the other, it locks.

Time slips away from my hand,
like calloused fingers trying to hold sand.

The crossroads' clock struck thrice,
and the others ran,
as if cat to a mice.

And once again,

I stand here on this crossroad,
alone and afraid,
with my heart belonging to no one path,
and my soul having no one fate.

So I move to where all cats chase mice,
not caring of my unbound mind's demise.

18. Petals of the Past

"All I am is an old rose,
forgotten between the pages of different lives.
Like all flowers, once bloom and wither,
all love must grow in our hands,
and like dust, slither."
she whispered to the old withering garden,
which once had bloomed like Eden.

- an extract from a future book

19. A Crimson Liberation

I plunge a knife in my heart,

gasping and whimpering as I hold the blade.

In agony, I retch—

a crimson pool beneath me forms.

A taste of metal from my mouth it reeks.

I twist the blade,

and in pain, I scream.

It hurts, hurts so much,

yet never reaching the hurt of your thousand slicing words.

I beg death to end this pain.

He laughed, his voice mocking in my brain.

I take the blade out,

my heart pouring her emotions

through the seeping blood.

And in the tainted mirror,

I see a girl—free and undone.

20. Tell Me, My Lord

What do you know of a heartache, my lord?
What do you know of yearning?
Of a pain that ignites a fire,
which burns and soothes my cold broken soul at the same time.
As if it's mending all of my cracks in my heart,
and yet the one melting it all away,
seeping the iron in my veins,
poisoning my body—
my heart in a cage.
It's not that you don't know of love and its joy,
but do you know of being like that once-old, used toy?
To give all of your heart and to be returned in pieces...
So I ask once again—
What do you know of a heartache, my lord?
What do you know of yearning?

21. The Dinner I Dread

A table for four
And a mouth of three.
A throbbing heart of two,
One head hanging down I see.

Expectations served on a platter,
The dinner turned to a clatter.
When did I start to fear this time?
Trying to get away, selling all my dimes.

The food which touched my lips
Hid the blood from my ears—it drips.
With a stuttering tongue, I ask for a spoon,
And there comes the question of how did I spend my noon.

A heavy heart starts to sag,
Knowing it never gave you a chance to brag.
A table of four
Turns out to be a nightmare of one.

A pinch of salt is all it needs
To make all of my sore wounds again undone.

22. Veins of Silence

You keep a knife to my throat
and ask me if my heart is beating fast.
My tongue stutters, my eyes dart—
but my heart, oh, my heart,
it climbs up to my throat,
choking me on words
perhaps I'll never speak.
So yes, it does beat fast,
but not from dull fear—
rather, from scarlet alphabets unspoken.
And at last, they do flow,
not through my lips,
but through the lining
cut on my neck,
spilling from the veins.

23. The Overlooked Bloom

In a field of roses, and tulips, and lilies,

I am a wildflower, surrounded by grass.

So when you say I'm beautiful,

Who would you pick if you looked up at the mass?

24. Yesterday's Remnants

Days and days pass,
and I look behind to see—
the yesterday I once lived
has drifted years away,
its laughter still echoing
in the halls of memory lane.
How did time slip like sand?
It was just there,
right in my hand.
What should I do now?
Do I start to pick each grain,
or let it go,
set free in an unknown land?
Days and days pass,
and I look behind to see—
yesterday was beautiful,
even if unplanned.

25. A Heart of Blackened Pages

"If you tear my heart open,
you'll see the black ink of pages,
describing my pain ever so poetically."
she whispered—
to the abyss that once had been a friend.

26. A Thousand Little Passions

She is passionate

about old Bollywood movies,

which make her laugh and cry.

She is passionate

about classical songs,

which she can't sing, no matter the try.

She is passionate

about books she might

never write.

She is passionate

about the poems in her heart—

they reside.

She is passionate

about colors she will never paint.

She is passionate

about her stretch marks and scars,

no matter the taint.

She is passionate

about pages with ink,

which will never fade.

She is passionate

about the flowers,

under God's feet they're laid.
She is passionate
about the sky and its bounds.
She is passionate
about the kids in the playground.
She is passionate
about the coffee she drinks.
She is passionate
about the thoughts she thinks.
She is passionate
about the bangles she wears.
She is passionate
about pain and its tears.
She is passionate
about the music of nature.
She is passionate
about animals,
no matter the creature.
She is passionate
about the people she meets.
She is passionate
about one's merit and deeds.
She is passionate
about the love she gives
but never receives.
She is passionate
about the trees and their leaves.

She is passionate

about everything one can say,

because God did not create rules

to find passion and love in a single way.

27. The Child I Chained

In my heart resides a prisoner,
The child within—the inner.
She loved to laugh and play,
Maybe giggle and sway.

But now she's locked,
Not in a pretty cage,
Where there is no hope—
Like labor with no wage.

My sweet girl, this world is not a dollhouse,
We couldn't afford to let you out.
In the bitter madness, you would be lost,
Like a shoe or a sock.

You would get hurt, sweet pie,
For monsters here, they lie.
So I must hide you behind bars of steel,
I can't give you the wheel.

Forgive me if you can,
For the love we both will lack.

28. Heartbeats of Longing

You kept your head on my heart,
You told me my heart was beating fast.
Let it beat, darling. Let it beat fast,
For you don't know how it survives on days without you.
You don't know how my lonely heart lasts.

29. A Niche in the Ashes

I thought I finally found my niche,
One that was only mine to keep.
But alas, I was disappointed—
I should've known things drift in deep sleeps.

I waited for you for years,
Like an eclipse—how the sun and moon near.
I had been waiting for an eternity,
Longing for a touch, a glance...
Yet you played with my body,
Never giving my heart a chance.

If this is my destiny, my fate,
I wish this stupid heart had fallen a little late.
I thought we were meant to be,
Thought the stars had knitted us together.
But I didn't know my summer peace
Could be destroyed by little bad weather.

The book of love we wrote was set on fire,
And now I cannot find the ashes or the pyre.
There was never an ending, no closure it seemed—
You just left as I wept and dreamed.

So this story was left incomplete,
And I went again to find my niche.

30. Of Thorns and Shields

Love in its purest form is agony.

Maybe that's why every rose has a thorn.

Maybe that's why in love and battle, armours are worn.

One shields the bones, and one shields the heart.

One is removed at the end of a battle, and one worn at the start.

31. The Ache of Belonging

Nobody is mine—

Maybe that's why I lose everything I find.

Maybe I hold it too tight, too loose,

Maybe that's why I'm someone no one will ever choose.

And it hurts,

It aches my soul,

As tears leave my eyes,

And my parched lips wait to be whole.

When shall I have someone I can call mine?

Who'll love me, no matter the time?

Just once, I could kiss calloused hands,

Just once, my heart could bloom on barren land.

Nobody is mine—

Maybe that's why I lose everything I find.

32. Drenched in Despair

I am nothing but a self-pit of wallowing misery,
And I am everything deemed of that title.

33. The Garden of My Woes

Every day, I find a thorn
In the garden of my woes—
Still, I walk barefoot, on my tippy toes.

I search for the flower I once had sown,
But all the thorns the garden has shown.

So I wonder—do I burn this all?
Do I let my rage's wildfire consume it tall?

But no—
The faint smell of roses still lingers from the past,
And I forget the scars of thorns on my hands, they last.

Nostalgia once again consumes my woes,
And my tears reflect the eerie of the garden as it grows.

I wait for that one rose to bloom—
Maybe I'll wait a hundred years or till the noon.

So, for now, I set the thorns aside,
Waiting in the garden of my woes -

under the midnight moonlight.

34. A Poet's Alchemy

I'm a Poet

I am bound

To turn the warmth of a matchstick

Into the ashes of a pyre.

A drop of water

Into the thirst of an ocean.

And the pain of a cut

Into the ache of a dying soul.

35. When Beauty Belongs Elsewhere

And if I hear the word "*beauty*,"

He comes to my mind.

He is art in himself,

Like the one he creates as he writes, he sings, he draws.

His ink belongs to his dear,

No, that dear is not me,

No matter how much I wish to be.

And it is a forbidden, unrequited love, I presume,

For he is no less mortal,

And I'm a foolish girl.

There is a glow on his face,

A spark in his eyes as he speaks of her,

As he speaks the words he wrote for his dear.

And we both are too far,

There is no land which can bring us near.

My hands hastily move on paper as I think of him,

And if he knew me, what could we have been?

36. Ashes of the Past

I am standing at the ashes of my past self.
I don't know if this is good or bad,
Right or wrong.
I just know this is how I belong.

It wasn't easy burning the pyre,
I was scared of what now will acquire.
It wasn't just me who got burnt,
It was everything I held so dear, was turned.

It was the dreams and my insecurities & fears,
Big like the streams which were so near.
I knew this was written in fate,
I knew my past needed to break.
'Cause to build houses, you need to put something at stake.

So here I am, a new body, a new soul.
I hope this one is different, it's not cold.
I smear the ashes on my forehead,
It's something not completely dead.

I still have something lingering behind,
But now my fears & strengths are lined.

These ashes are my lessons and life in a pot.
This new self will carry it, it yet has to learn a lot.

I am new, yet I am old.
My past was a treasure box,
and now my present will unlock the gold.

37. Of Scars and Silence

I wish that I was enough,
and maybe the world wasn't this rough.

For the pain inflicted on my skin were none,
for the scars to be other than mine.

I wish this world wouldn't laugh at my pain
and say it's fine.

I wish this world could be a little kind,
so it wouldn't be so difficult
for diamonds to find.

38. Seeing the Ordinary Anew

"*The ordinary are not beautiful*," he said.
I guess he has never seen the wildflowers
in my grandma's backyard.

Because when you look at them,
there is a part you foresee—
the part that blooms even on the coldest day,
the part that grows
without needing someone else to stay.

Yes, you see them everywhere,
they're easy to find,
but they, too, are beautiful—
always left behind.

Just because they are not rare,
you pick another without a care.

If you just look closely at the "ordinary,"
you'll find them pretty too.
Every fragrance, every leaf,

every petal is different for me and you.

You might see the thorn it bears,
but I'll see a little bug's home.
When I see a wildflower,
I see strength and beauty earned.

It doesn't matter if they are ordinary to the world.

39. My Moon and Stars

Even though you don't feel beautiful,
my poems and I look at you
the way the stars look at the moon.

There may be a thousand other things
that shine brighter than you,
but to me, you are my only source of light.

I wait for the sun to set,
for dusk to arrive—
so I can see all I want,
giving my heart strength to survive.

You may have spots you wish to cover,
but they, too, add to your beauty—
showing parts of you left to discover.

My poems and I are your secret lover,
and I promise you,
we love like no other.

Even though you will never know
that you're my moon and I'm your star,

I'll still love you
and look at you from afar.

40. A Life Outside My Window

All my friends are having fun,
and I'm stuck inside four walls.
They all meet and live their lives,
while I'm here, trying to be a know-it-all.

It's not that I don't know what fun is—
I want to enjoy and feel some bliss,
but I'm scared to see what I'll miss.

I don't know if they actually like me
or just pretend to play along.
They post their stories together,
while I stay alone with a sad song.

I'm always the first to leave an event,
like a message never read but sent.
I know no one will miss my presence—
in my life, loneliness has left its essence.

I'm scared I'll have no stories to tell,
and my kids will only know of my tears and their well.

41. The Song You Made of Me

If the idea of letting me go
was so painful,
then why did you play along?
Why did you stop me from everything?
Why did you make me this sad song?

You shattered the things
I brought to you in my hands,
then you wonder why my heart
is like the barren lands.

You believed that every flower is different,
but to you, I was a thorn.
So I made peace
to silence my loud mind,
but you destroyed it,
not letting me mourn.

You gave me happiness,
a cart filled with laughs,
but slowly, you tore my heart apart.

And now, I don't know where to go—
to myself right now,
or to the one I was before.

42. Eclipsed by Expectations

Sometimes I wonder—

Why is the moon pretty with its flaws and scars,

And I am not?

Why is the world so eager to fix me?

To cover what doesn't please their eyes,

And their price of beauty.

I often wonder—

Did God want me to be this way?

With my imperfections and flaws?

Did He want me to be like the moon—

To glow with my scars?

Or—

To remain in the darkness of the night,

Which the world wants me to be condemned to?

43. Splinters Of Hollow Sustenance

Fed with food,
starved of love.

Washed with water,
condemned to sins.

Dressed in clothes,
torn apart with words.

Drunk on water,
a thirst of poison.

A roof overhead,
a heart in a concrete cage.

Taught to speak,
left unheard.

Warmth of words,
cuts of noise.

A body of bones,

and a soul undone.

44. Verses of Vanishing

They say, "*If a poet loves you, you'll become immortal.*"
But maybe that's not so true.
For I
would burn all pages that held the possibility of you being mine.
I'll wipe all ink stains that wrote of my love once divine.
You'll live forever in my heart—
till eternity, my every breath is yours.
Everything you give me, I'll accept,
be it your joys or sorrows.
You aren't meant to be written on paper,
but engraved on stone.
But alas, my hands were too weak to hold you.
So I live with a pen in my hand
and a heart filled with love.

45. When the Curtains Never Rise

Drawing the curtains of my bedroom window,
I ponder what I could've become
if I were not caged
inside these four walls.

If I could go outside and shine bright,
but rather, I'm stuck in this dark plight.
How I wish to be a shining star,
but this dream of mine is locked away far.

I see people doing all the things
I was meant to be,
but I am so deep in this flight of misery
that not even a ray of my light they can see.

If only I had the chance, that opportunity—
maybe, just maybe, I would say I have an ability.

If I had been given a piano,
I would have created symphonies of heaven.
If I was given a voice,
I would help and lead them.

But alas, fate
has chosen my stage,
where there are no claps,
just tears like diamonds,
smudging my ink stains.

And I fear this weight
as my heart beats fast,
knowing this is my only chance
to prove my worth,
even if not my last.

Perhaps these dreams of mine
are like those stars in the sky,
which no one can find,
even if, like diamonds, they shine.

46. Beacon of Black Ink

The pitch night sky glows inside my heart.
The darkness of a storm gives a thunder,
keeping it from being torn apart.

The stains of my ink become my beacon,
giving my heart courage,
even when it is weakened and shaken.

The agony of my heart is written in black ink,
engraving every word upon my skin.
And this quality of mine
is not shared with my kin.

47. A Funeral for My Flesh

I bury my heart into the ground,
as I pray to the earth,
"*Oh mother, may you bloom my gift
into the softest yet strongest of creation.*"

I burn my body into ashes
and release them into the flowing rivers,
as they finally laugh and roam freely.

I trap my mind inside this long race called "*life*"
as it screams to be unchained.

And I drown my soul,
as it screams in agony,
mourning the loss of its wilderness.

As it sinks into the deep, bottomless lake of my horrors,
I sing a soft lullaby,
assuring her she will return—
even though I know she won't.

For I am now too lost, too deep,

and perhaps too broken
for freedom to yearn.

48. Wings Waiting in Silence

As my heart began to cradle grand dreams,
A weight held me back, or so it seemed.
I feared they were chains, cold and tight,
Dragging me far from the world's bright light.

So, I let the pen slip from my grasp,
Crumpled the pages, left them to clasp.
Silenced the words before they could rise,
Buried my dreams beneath fearful sighs.

But one day, I turned to see,
The truth that had been hiding in me.
And to my astonishment, bold and wide,
Were wings, not chains, resting at my side.

Wings as golden as words left unsaid,
As vast as the dreams I had long since shed.
They had been waiting all these years,
Through sleepless nights and silent tears.

No longer bound, no longer small,
I spread my wings, I heard the call.

With faith reborn and courage bright,
I soared toward the land of light.

49. What My Bones Remember

A child's sorrow
and a mother's heart.
A father's pain
and the beauty of art.
I carry it all
deep in my bones,
Every fiber of my being
knows this truth written on stone.
I carry parts of the people I love
and the parts of people I've hurt.
Their whispers linger in my veins,
their laughter stitched in joy and pains.
Their dreams still echo in my chest,
their silence lulls me into rest.
And though the past may weigh me down,
it molds my roots, it crowns my growth.

50. The Mirror and The Chase

And I hate every picture

I see of myself.

I see my eyes too small,

and my face too big.

I see my flaws and imperfections,

waiting for God to fix them.

And I do like laughing,

but I wonder if I'm too loud.

Is my body being liked?

Is my smile nice to someone if found?

I hate mirrors—

they reflect all my dreams of my heart on my face.

And then I go back again,

to the beauty of the world I chase.

51. Beyond the Smudged Paint Lines

Art was never meant to be perfect,
and neither were we.

Art was meant to be complete,
for our eyes to see,
but not to be chained in a set of rules to be.

It was supposed to be there,
with all its rawness and passion.
And we were supposed to live
a life not dedicated to some fashion.

Art was meant to please our souls,
not cover our flesh.
Art was meant to feel,
not bring us enmesh.

Art was meant to be immortal,
not by ink or paper,
but by settling in one's mind and bones.

Art was never meant to be perfect,

and neither were we.

So let go of these lines and squares of the world,
and leap into a world beyond the eyes we see.

The Final Curtain

About The Author

Kaashvi Nigam is a young aspiring poet who started writing 18 months ago when she was in grade 9.

From hating all kinds of books and book fairs to not being able to live without them and dragging her parents into every book stall she sees, times have certainly changed.

Kaashvi is a teenage writer who finds solace in words—both the worlds and hers—and believes that art can truly change the world.

So, do tell her, if her art changed you?

Instagram - @kaashvi.writes

Gmail - kaashvi.s.nigam@gmail.com

Epilouge

Ahh, the book has come to an end, I see.

Can you see it? The fire extinguishing, my friend?

I wonder if I can call you a friend, dear reader,

For now, you know a lot about me.

So, to return this favor, the exchange of words,

Spread them on my Instagram page – @kaashvi.writes / kaashvi.s.nigam@gmail.com

I bid you all goodbye,

Maybe one of joy or one of rue.

The moment you turn this page,

Our paths shall end,

Maybe not the same for our journey.

Farewell,

Kaashvi Nigam